The Song
A Lesson to Live By

by Ilene C. Herman

CITIOFBOOKS, INC.
3736 Eubank NE Suite A1
Albuquerque, NM 87111-3579
www.citiofbooks.com
Hotline: 1 (877) 389-2759
Fax: 1 (505) 930-7244

Ordering Information:
Quantity sales. Special discounts are available on quantity purchases by corporations, associations, and others. For details, contact the publisher at the address above.

Printed in the United States of America.

ISBN-13:   Softcover   979-8-89391-300-2
                    eBook   979-8-89391-301-9

Library of Congress Control Number: 2024918278

A playful baboon

Took out his bassoon

And made up a tune

On a morning in June

The sound reached the ear
Of a goat and a deer
And they sang loud and clear
So the whole world could hear

Then a Mother giraffe
And her wobbly-kneed calf
Joined in with a laugh
As their necks bent in half

Soon a chimp and a gnu
And a white cockatoo
Heard a cow give a "Moo"
And they sang along too

A wolf and a loon

Heard the wonderful tune

And they started to croon

In the forest at noon

A dog and a cat

And a bear and a bat

Cried, "We can sing that

With the pig and the rat"

Six snakes slithered by
And decided to try
To sing sweet and high
With a fox and a fly

The horse gave a "Neigh"
And the donkey a bray
And the lamb cried, "Hooray!
We will all sing today!"

Four fish swam single file

With a green crocodile

They splashed with a smile

As they all sang awhile

The baboon felt so proud

When he heard the big crowd

He smiled and he bowed

As he played extra loud

The owl took a drink

As she saw the sun sink

Her eyes went *blink-blink*

And she hooted, "I think …

The world is designed

So we're all different kinds

Different colors and minds

But each of us finds

That all the day long
We have sung the same song
So I'm sure I'm not wrong
We can all get along!"

About the Author

Ilene Weinberger grew up in Cleveland, Ohio where she won her first writing award in the fourth grade for an essay about America. Her skills as a writer were honed while writing greeting card verses for the American Greeting Card company as well as being a featured writer on her high school paper. While continuing to write her greeting cards, she graduated summa cum laude with a degree in Speech and Hearing Therapy from Western Reserve University in Cleveland. Her first professional job was an experimental program treating speech therapy problems working with first and second grade classes in southeastern Ohio and her success there developed into a permanent program.

Upon graduation, she also married her high school sweetheart, Irwin Herman. After he finished his medical school, residency program and Army service they made the decision to move west as California beckoned. After settling in the San Francisco Bay Area, Ilene became enamored of California and Native American history and she embarked on a career of studying and writing about these topics. She obtained a master's degree in Applied History from Holy Names College in Oakland and has published numerous papers accepted by the Bancroft Library of UC Berkeley as well as commentaries in some of the local newspapers. When she became active in helping form and becoming part of several writers' groups, her writing style changed as she began writing more verses and short stories as well as plays, essays and travel articles as the couple travelled the world over the years.

Many of her stories were based on fictionalized real events that had been part of her life, but Ilene also had a knack for creating spontaneous tales appealing to children as her grandchildren began to arrive, which was very helpful on long driving trips. Many of the characters, as well as the plots and locations evolved as the little ones would suggest specific items they wanted to hear. Ilene has also been published in anthologies such as *Thema* and *Chicken Soup for the Soul* among others. She was always a strong supporter of many social issues, especially those supporting children's issues and policies, and it was this that I believe prompted the creation of the theme of this book, namely that, early education of our children can help solve the divisiveness and hate that is plaguing the world today, because our future really is in their hands.

After a sudden illness, Ilene died after sixty-five years of marriage at the age of eighty-seven. This book is being published as a memorial to her efforts and her beliefs. I hope you and your little ones enjoy the story.

www.ingramcontent.com/pod-product-compliance
Lightning Source LLC
Chambersburg PA
CBHW041531120626
46551CB00018B/2648